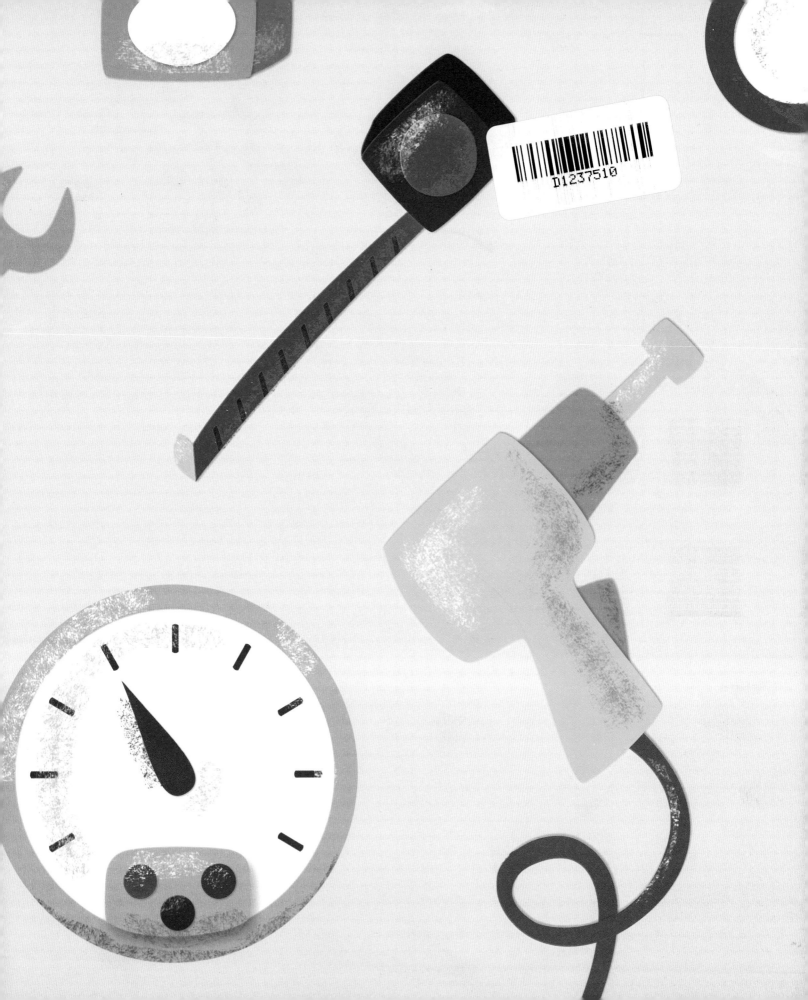

NASCAR 1-2-3s GLOSSARY

adjustments—The changes and fine-tuning made to the car before and during the race.

Chase for the NASCAR Sprint Cup—The final ten races in the NASCAR season, in which the top twelve drivers—those with the most points after the first twenty-six races—compete for the championship. In the book it is referred to as the "championship chase."

crew chief—The person who oversees the pit crew from the pit box, acting as an equivalent to a head coach.

cylinders—Where the combustion takes place that powers the race car. Engines in the NASCAR Sprint Cup Series cars have eight cylinders, each with a piston inside that moves up and down.

Daytona bank—Refers to the rather steep thirty-one-degree banking at the massive two-and-a-half-mile Daytona International Speedway.

different tracks—Refers to the twenty-two different racetracks in the NASCAR Sprint Cup Series.

fifty greatest drivers—A list of the all-time greatest NASCAR drivers, though it may differ depending on whom you ask.

first NASCAR win—Took place on the Daytona Beach and Road Course on February 15, 1948. The winner was Red Byron. However, the first NASCAR "Strictly Stock" (currently NASCAR Sprint Cup Series) race win belongs to

Jim Roper, who won at Charlotte Fairgrounds Speedway on June 19, 1949.

five points—The number of points a NASCAR driver earns for leading at least one lap of a race.

forty-three drivers—The number of drivers who qualify for each NASCAR Sprint Cup Series race.

front-runners—The group of cars leading the race.

Keep digging—An expression that means "keep trying your best."

lap—Each full trip around the track.

NASCAR—National Association for Stock Car Auto Racing.

over-the-wall pit crew members—The only people allowed over the wall to work on a car during a pit stop. They are the (1) jack man, (2) front tire changer, (3) rear tire changer, (4) gas man, (5) catch can man, (6) front tire carrier, and (7) rear tire carrier.

pack—A group of race cars bunched together as they move around the track.

stickers—Another name for brand-new tires. The name refers to the manufacturer's stickers that are found on the surface of all new tires.

two hundred wins—Driver Richard Petty holds the all-time NASCAR Sprint Cup Series record with 200 wins.

Paul DuBois Jacobs **and** Jennifer Swender

Illustrated by

Aaron Zenz

GIBBS SMITH
TO ENRICH AND INSPIRE HUMANKIND

Salt Lake City | Charleston | Santa Fe | Santa Barbara

Readers, start your engines.

1-2-3!

Rev up your NASCAR numbers with me!

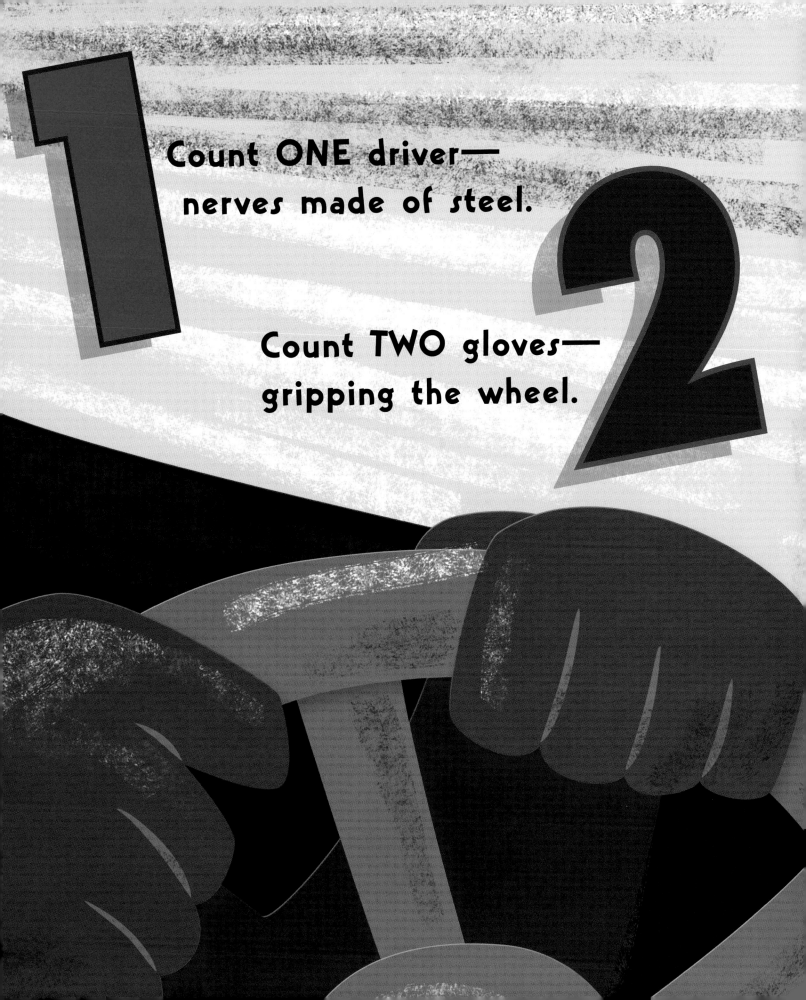

Count ONE driver—
nerves made of steel.

Count TWO gloves—
gripping the wheel.

3

Count THREE fans—
doing their part.

Count FOUR stickers—
ready to start.

Count FIVE points—
when you lead a lap.

Count SIX letters—
on the crew chief's cap.

Count SEVEN crew members—
ready to jump.

Count **EIGHT** cylinders— starting to pump.

8

Count NINE front-runners— pulling into place.

Count **TEN** races—
in the championship chase.

Just keep digging—safely 'round the bend.
Let's keep counting—now by tens!

Count **TWENTY** teams—
    that make up the pack.
        Twenty plus two—
            for each different track.

THIRTY plus one—for a Daytona bank.

FORTY plus three—
all the drivers in
the ranks.

FIFTY greatest drivers.
Count yourself in!

Count SIXTY years—
since the first NASCAR win.

SEVENTY, EIGHTY—miles per hour.

Pushing past NINETY. Feel the power!

Make your adjustments—
ONE HUNDRED
different tools.

100

GO FOR 200!

200 WINS!

TWO HUNDRED wins—
the record that rules!

So many races with HUNDRED in their names:
THREE HUNDRED, FOUR HUNDRED—none
are the same.

FIVE HUNDRED, SIX HUNDRED miles around.
Feel the rush and hear the sound!

1,000,000

MILLIONS and
MILLIONS and
MILLIONS of fans!

Shut down your engine.
The race is done.
In NASCAR numbers—
you're number ONE!

A is for Alex—you're #1.
—Paul and Jennifer

For my father-in-law, the Revvin' Reverend Gerry Wyma
—Aaron Zenz

First Edition
13 12 11 10 09   5 4 3 2 1

Published by

Gibbs Smith

P.O. Box 667
Layton, Utah 84041

Orders: 1.800.835.4993
www.gibbs-smith.com

Designed by Mark Wummer
Printed and bound in China
Gibbs Smith books are printed on either recycled,
100% post consumer waste, or FSC certified papers.

Library of Congress Cataloging-in-Publication Data

Library of Congress Control Number: 2008931445

ISBN 13: 978-1-4236-0477-8
ISBN 10: 1-4236-0477-6

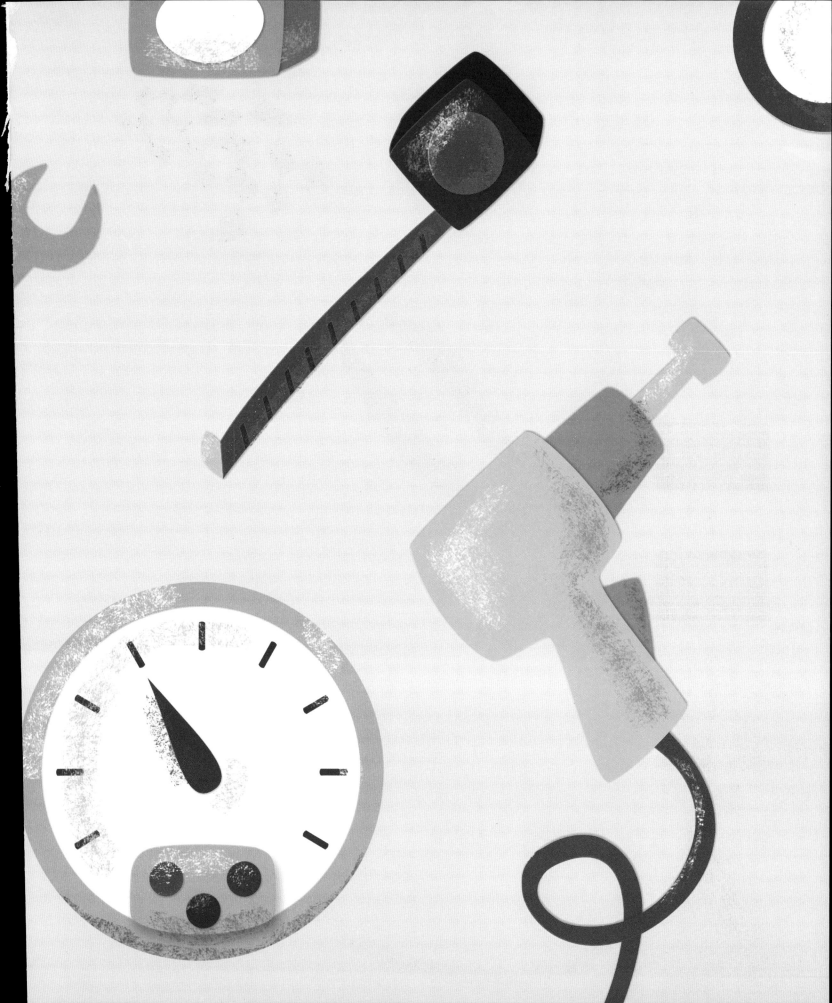